Original title:
The Salt of the Earth

Copyright © 2025 Creative Arts Management OÜ
All rights reserved.

Author: Sophia Kingsley
ISBN HARDBACK: 978-1-80581-616-4
ISBN PAPERBACK: 978-1-80581-143-5
ISBN EBOOK: 978-1-80581-616-4

Strands of Solidarity

In the kitchen where chaos reigns,
Spices hit the floor, the cat complains.
A pinch of laughter, a dash of cheer,
As we whip up memories year after year.

No recipe's right, just a blend of fun,
Adding a joke as we stir and run.
Tables adorned with mix-ups galore,
Taste-testing fails that we all adore.

Potato chips sprinkled on our stew,
Who knew that was something we could do?
A feast of giggles, a buffet of puns,
United we munch, while our chaos runs.

So gather 'round for this quirky pot,
In this kitchen, we've got plenty of hot.
With sidelined messes and smiles so wide,
In this kitchen of ours, we're all bona fide!

Seasons of Earth

Springtime blooms with sneaky bees,
Pollen counts bring us to our knees.
Summer's warmth, a sunburned jest,
Sipping lemonade, we try our best.

Autumn leaves like boisterous shouts,
Sweaters on—oh, how it pouts!
Winter slips in with icy glee,
Hot chocolate jokes as warm as can be.

Tides of Texture

Waves do dance with sandy grace,
Footprints vanish, just like space.
Crabs in suits with claws so proud,
They pinch the tourists, yell aloud!

Seashells giggle, secrets to tell,
Whispers of treasures, who knows as well?
Each tide pulls in delight and cheer,
Just watch your toes—they disappear!

The Earth's Gift

A muffin's crumb, a floury face,
Kneading dough at a merry pace.
Eggs roll by, a breakfast ball,
Pancakes stack up, having a brawl!

Herbs sprout leaves like pranks on plates,
Garlic breath that no one rates.
Nature's bounty, all on parade,
Eating veggies is quite the charade!

Vitality in Grains

Rice and beans in a big stew pot,
Mixing flavors—oh, what a lot!
Corn on the cob with butter flow,
Eating great—like a fun show!

Bread so fresh, it jumps with glee,
Crumbling crumbs, as wild as can be.
Oats in cookies, a playful trick,
Vitality laughs, oh what a kick!

Threads of Tradition

In Grandma's kitchen, flour flies high,
While the old cat plans its next sly spy.
Baking bread, a science gone wild,
With a pinch of mischief, she's just a child.

Recipes sticky, hands covered in goo,
She swears the secret's in her old shoe!
A dash of chaos, a sprinkle of cheer,
Whisking up laughter, that's why we're here.

Memories in Flavor

Oh, the joys of a Sunday roast!
The smoke alarms whistle—oh, what a boast!
We gather around as the fire blares,
And Mama just swears she's the one who cares.

Pie crusts crumbled, but laughter prevails,
While Uncle Joe tells his outlandish tales.
Each bite is treasured, memories unfold,
Every spoonful tastes like stories retold.

Grounded Generations

In the garden, we dig with glee,
Searching for carrots that run wild and free.
Grandpa's wisdom mixed with dirt,
He claims its magic, but I'm just hurt.

Potatoes sprouting in our backyard,
Growing like laughter, both joyful and hard.
We plant our dreams beneath the sun's glow,
With roots so deep, they're bound to grow.

Essence of Generations

Mismatched socks march in a line,
Dance around the pantry—oh, what a sign!
Cousins juggle spices, a delightful mess,
While grandpa's stories, he can't quite express.

Stirring the pot of our crazy past,
With half-baked ideas, we're unsurpassed.
Every flavor shared is a joke well-told,
And in every bite, new memories unfold.

Savoring Simple Truths

In a world where flavors blend,
Even bland has its own trend.
A sprinkle here, a dash nearby,
Who knew the plain could make us fly?

On Tuesday, chips flew off the shelf,
There's always room for one more elf!
With popcorn smiles and salty cheer,
We dance with crumbs, our hearts sincere.

Crystals in the Soil

A garden patch with no straight lines,
Hiding treasures like old wines.
The carrots giggle, beets won't share,
While radishes flaunt their rooty hair.

Worms roll through dirt like they own the place,
Shaking their tails in a muddy race.
With peas doing cartwheels, oh what a sight,
Even the beans think they're out of sight!

Bounty of Belonging

In the kitchen, chaos reigns supreme,
With too much spice, we squawk and scream.
A recipe calls for just a pinch,
But we scoop handfuls with a happy clinch.

Friends gather round, they're fearless chefs,
Tasting mishaps like educated guess.
With burnt toast tales and laughter loud,
We feast together, a merry crowd.

Tides of Humility

The waves roll in, a cheeky tease,
Salt and sea, a fragrant breeze.
We dip our toes in, glossed with glee,
While seagulls shout, 'Come join the spree!'

Each grain of sand a tiny tale,
Of buckets, castles, flip-flop fail.
In foamy laughter, we find our place,
As nature's humor leaves a trace.

Essence of Resilience

Life's tough, like jerky that's dried,
Yet we chew through the challenges, wide-eyed.
We bounce back, a rubbery prank,
Turning sour days into laughs at the bank.

Got grit like a chef's secret spice,
Sautéing struggles with a dash that's nice.
When plans flop, we just sauté,
With laughter and snacks, we find our way.

Nature's Infusion

In the garden, veggies throw a dance,
Tomatoes twirl like they've found romance.
Root veggies laugh underground, they say,
"Who knew carrots could party this way?"

Basil's fresh with a zesty flair,
While rosemary's busy in its fragrant chair.
Herbs gossip, sharing their secrets bright,
Flavors unite, and everything feels right.

The Flavor of Community

Neighbors gather, pots in hand,
Cooking up joy, that's our grand plan.
Sharing recipes, laughter, and bread,
Who knew a soup could get us all fed?

In this melting pot, we stir and stir,
Every line's a joke, and everyone's a blur.
With laughter like spice, we simmer all night,
Serving up love, everything's just right.

Cradles of Nourishment

Whisking eggs like a maestro's flair,
Baking bread with the utmost care.
Sourdough giggles rise in the pan,
"Feed me butter, and I'm your biggest fan!"

In the kitchen, chaos is true art,
Flour flies like confetti from the start.
Spatulas spin like they've lost their way,
But every mishap brings joy to the day.

Beneath the Surface

In a little town, folks love to dine,
The chef sneezes, adds a pinch of brine.
Suddenly the soup, it starts to shine,
Boiling laughter, oh that's divine!

Jars of pickles dance on the shelf,
They whisper, 'We've got to spice ourselves!'
A salty tale of flavors untold,
In our kitchen, the stories unfold.

Flavorful Footprints

Walking through the market, oh what a treat,
I tripped on a burrito, landed on my feet!
Chili con carne, a slippery dance,
My taste buds crying, 'Give us a chance!'

Cabbage rolls rolling down the green hill,
With mustard on top, they were never still.
Each step I take, a flavorful mess,
Spilling my lunch? Now that's progress!

Unyielding Elements

A pinch of salt and a dash of play,
Turnip tops twirl in a cheeky ballet.
They laugh at the pasta getting all sauced,
As they tango on plates, they can't be tossed!

The spices engage in a verbal spat,
Cinnamon pouts, says, 'Look at that!
I'm sweet like a hug, why's pepper so fine?'
They shake it out loud, what a zesty line!

Alchemy of Life

In the cauldron, stew bubbles with glee,
Carrots laugh, they say, 'Look at me!'
Onions croon, shedding layers of smiles,
With each chop, they're shedding their trials.

Garlic dances slick on the wooden board,
Chopping away till the whole gang's bored.
In this kitchen, humor's the vital spice,
Stirring up joy, oh how nice!

Culinary Kinship

In the kitchen, laughter spills,
With pots that dance and spoons that thrill.
A dash of chaos, a pinch of zest,
Family feasts are simply the best.

Grandma's secret, a wink and a grin,
Add extra garlic, and let the fun begin!
Caught in a tussle with flour in the air,
Who knew cooking could cause such a scare?

Laughter rising, like dough in a bowl,
As cousins roll pasta, we all play a role.
Burnt edges? No problem, it's all a game!
We serve up love, that's what we claim!

Tangible Heritage

In old jars sit stories, preserved with care,
Pickled memories of laughter we share.
A spoonful of history with every bite,
Cousins in the kitchen, what a delightful sight!

Recipes passed down like heirlooms of gold,
Each one a tale that's patiently told.
A swirl of spices, a giggle or two,
Heritage served on a plate for a view!

From granddad's stew to Auntie's sweet pie,
The flavors of family make our hearts fly.
Food's just a vessel for laughter and cheer,
With each tasty story, we hold family dear.

Simple Elegance

A table set softly, with humor in mind,
Each dish a jest, an experience blind.
Salad so crisp, it might just jump,
Dressing so slippery, it adds to the thump!

We toast with soda, not wine in a glass,
Giggling at folks with their fancy class.
Mealtime magic, like a whimsical show,
As we try to dine while juggling a dough!

Napkins as capes, we're superheroes tonight,
Fighting off boredom with forks held up tight.
In the art of eating, there's fun and finesse,
Simple and silly, we surely are blessed.

Layers of Existence

Stacked like a cake, our lives intertwine,
Each layer a giggle, each bite a sign.
From crumbs of chaos to frosting delight,
We feast on the moments that make life feel right.

Life's lasagna of laughter, with rules we ignore,
Saucy confessions and anecdotes galore.
Baking mishaps, a casserole craze,
Our kitchen a circus, each meal a maze!

With friends gathered round, the joy overflows,
Like whipped cream clouds or cupcake prose.
Layers of life, all sprinkled with glee,
In our culinary world, we just let it be!

Shards of Resilience

When life gives you lemons, make a pie,
But skip the crust, just let it fly!
A lopsided smile with a touch of cheese,
Twisting absurdity with genuine ease.

Flour on the ceiling, jam on the floor,
If baking's a chore, then let's all snore.
A cake that flops is still cake indeed,
Grab a fork and dive in, it's all we need!

Palates of the Common

Dinner's a circus, the table's the tent,
With mismatched chairs, there's lots of content.
Spaghetti flinging like confetti in the air,
Watch out for that meatball, it's flying with flair!

Who needs fine dining, we're kings of the mess,
Sprinkle some chaos, it's all for the best.
A toast with our mugs, filled with soda pop,
Laughter fills silence; let the good times drop!

Grounded in Grace

In the yard we plan a garden so grand,
With weeds as our friends, we give them a hand.
A carrot parade, oh what a sight,
Dancing with radishes, all through the night!

We dig in the dirt for treasures and gems,
And plant silly plans, along with our stems.
Muddy shoes tell tales of laughter and fun,
Nature's a jester, always on the run!

Verdant Foundations

Beneath the surface, the roots do play,
Cheering each other in the silliest way.
A beet high-fives a potato, so stout,
While onions giggle, no worries, no doubt.

The lawn's a stage where the critters perform,
With ants in tuxedos, it's quite the norm.
Grasshoppers croon in a playful duet,
Nature's a comedy we can't forget!

Nature's Palette

In fields where colors blend and sway,
The daisies laugh, come out to play.
The trees wear coats of vibrant hues,
While squirrels sneak snacks, it's old news.

Bright flowers gossip, sharing their cheer,
While bees play matchmaker, buzzing near.
The sun, a painter with a warm brush,
Giggles echo in the blooms' soft hush.

Earth's Sugary Bounty

Beneath the soil, a treasure chest,
Carrots and radishes wear their best.
Potatoes hide, oh what a stunt!
While sweet beets smile, "We're on the hunt!"

Grapes pop bubbles, sipping the sun,
Cucumbers chuckle, saying, "We're fun!"
Each veggie's dance on the garden floor,
Is a joke that nature has in store.

Remedies of the Soil

Digging deep for a quirky cure,
Worms wiggle on, oh so demure.
With every scoop, they raise a cheer,
Giant radishes, hidden near!

Garlic whispers with a wink and nod,
"Foul breath? Just call on me, oh God!"
Herbs throw parties in fragrant delight,
While thyme tickles the tongue, what a sight!

Nourishing Connections

Roots entwined in a dance of fate,
Sharing gossip about what's on plate.
The tomatoes blush, feeling the squeeze,
While zucchini jokes, "I'm a veggie tease!"

Beans and corn in a charming race,
Compete for sun, a friendly face.
Together they make a gang so bold,
Their laughter in harvest stories told.

Resonance of Roots

In the garden, worms groove,
Twisting and wriggling, they move.
Plants gossip with a chuckle,
In the dirt, they form a huddle.

Sunflowers wear shades, looking cool,
While the carrots join at the pool.
Roots high-five when rains begin,
Nature's party, let the fun spin!

Dandelions dance, a small bouquet,
Calling bees for a blurry buffet.
Every creature's laughter light,
In the soil, joy takes flight!

Digging deep with a spoon, oh dear,
A potato yells, "It's cramped down here!"
But to each their quirky place,
Life finds rhythm with a funny face.

Grains of Life

On the farm where grains unite,
Wheat whispers, "I'm a tasty sight."
Corn pops, laughing at the joke,
"It's all about the kernel yoke!"

Rice is humble, quite refined,
Sharing tales of the fields combined.
Barley brags, "I'm in a brew,"
Crafting drinks just for you!

The oats roll around in a whirl,
Jumping high without a pearl.
In every grain, a story's spun,
Harvest laughter, oh what fun!

Dancing atop a pancake hot,
Syrup's sticky — it's a culinary plot!
Pasta twirls in a saucy embrace,
The grains unite, a feast we ace!

Essence of Nature

Nature giggles with every breeze,
Tickling leaves, swaying with ease.
Trees wear hats made of bark,
While squirrels scheme like a park lark.

Rivers splish, splash, twist and turn,
With fish who think they're here to learn.
Clouds drift by, they're quite the clowns,
Making shapes, wearing fuzzy gowns!

Mountains grumble, "We're very tall!"
But the valleys laugh, they have a ball.
Nature's essence, a funny blend,
Where life's quirks never quite end!

In a grove where critters meet,
A party vibes, it's oh so sweet.
Every inch a playful tease,
Nature's laughter floats like the breeze!

Salted Whispers

Sprinkled tales on foods divine,
Salt shimmies, saying, "I'm fine!"
Popcorn skips into a bowl,
Every kernel plays a role.

Pizzas giggle with crispy crust,
Flavors swirl, it's a must!
A margarita whispers back,
"Just sprinkle me, I'm on the track!"

In every pantry, a story brews,
With shy spices in bright hues.
From soups that bubble to chips that crunch,
Every taste, a playful punch!

So let's toast with a salted cheer,
Celebrating flavors far and near.
In every grain, a tastier jest,
Cooking up life, we feel the best!

Heartbeats of the Earth

In a world where laughter reigns,
And joy flows through our veins,
Like sprinkles on a donut sweet,
We find the rhythm in our feet.

Burping whales and dancing trees,
Tickling breezes, buzzing bees,
With every giggle of the sun,
We stir the pot of life's great fun.

The clouds on high, they crack a smile,
While rainbows jest and linger awhile,
Each heart thumps wildly, full of cheer,
As Mother Earth winks with a leer.

So let's toast to our silly fate,
And laugh aloud, it's never late,
Because in this grand, absurd dance,
We twirl and swirl in joy's romance.

Essence of Progress

With every step in shoes so bright,
We chase our dreams from morn to night,
Inventing gadgets, oh what a sight,
Making progress feel just right.

We flip our phones like pancakes hot,
And share our lunch in the latest plot,
With hashtags soaring to a new high,
Crafting laughter as we fly by.

Those sponsored ads, a sight to see,
Promising bliss in a cup of tea,
While robots laugh at each bad pun,
We toast to progress, just for fun!

In this crazy race, don't lose your hat,
Embrace the quirks, and that is that,
'Cause life's a journey, not a test,
So sing and dance, and be your best!

Infusions of Heritage

Grandma's stew, oh what a taste,
A sprinkle of history, not a waste,
We gather 'round with tales galore,
Every spoonful opens a door.

Traditions dance like fireflies bright,
Jokes and jests by the candlelight,
With every sip, we taste the past,
A flavorful banquet that's built to last.

From time-worn recipes full of flair,
To quirky dances that fill the air,
Heritage brings us silly delight,
With every laugh, our spirits take flight.

So raise a glass to those who came,
Their wacky ways ignite the flame,
In every bite and every cheer,
We forge a bond that's crystal clear.

Earth's Seasoned Embrace

When winter's kiss brings frosty glee,
We bundle up like a hot cup of tea,
Spring tickles buds that bloom so bright,
While summer bakes us in pure delight.

Leaves in autumn play peek-a-boo,
Swirling down like a jazzy crew,
With every season's wacky prank,
We dance through life, our spirits rank.

Embrace the quirks, the nature's jest,
A playful breeze, a feathered guest,
'Cause every hug from the great outdoors,
Affects our heart, opens new doors.

So let's toast to the wild and free,
With laughter shared 'neath the old oak tree,
In every season's merry chase,
We find our joy in Earth's warm embrace.

Threads of Humanity

In a world where quirks abound,
Little threads keep us all bound.
From shoelaces lost to socks that don't match,
Life's tapestry weaves a fun patch.

With every mix-up, there's a laugh,
Like cooking soup without the half,
Of ingredients needed, the taste's real sly,
Oh look, it's just a noodle pie!

We trip on jokes like mismatched shoes,
Dance to the tune of our daily blues.
Life's a circus, we juggle our dreams,
While juggling balls that burst at the seams.

So here's to the fun, in lost and found,
To friendships woven, life's merry round.
In every twist, a chuckle will rise,
Tie it together with a bow of surprise!

Nature's Remnants

In the garden, weeds wear crowns,
While daisies shout, 'We won't frown!'
Nature chuckles at grown-up plans,
As squirrels steal nuts from our hands.

Bright blooms prance, with colors loud,
While bugs march in, quite proud.
A flower's scent leads a bee astray,
Don't follow that rogue; it's gone haywire today!

Leaves joke about the winds that blow,
'Take your hats, it's time to go!'
The trees are whispering secrets sweet,
About the acorns that wander on feet.

So laugh with the breeze, and dance with the ants,
Life is a party in muddy pants.
When nature plays, we all must cheer,
For the remnants of laughter are always near!

Tincture of Time

Tick-tock goes the clock of fate,
With every second, we celebrate.
Time's a potion, with bubbling glee,
A splash of chaos, a dash of tea.

In the past, I may have slipped,
On banana peels that fate has whipped.
With moments lost and memories gained,\nTime's a
playground where fun is maintained.

Future plans in scramble mode,
Like socks that hide on a laundry road.
We measure time in laughter's beat,
Or how long we wait for food to eat!

So toast to the moments, both silly and grand,
In this tincture of time, take a stand.
Embrace the absurd, let hilarity churn,
For each tick-tock brings a new turn!

Foundations of Flavor

In kitchens where laughter brews,
Flavors collide, dance in hues.
An onion's cry brings giggles near,
'Chop me quicker, shed a tear!'

Spices jostle in jars like friends,
Each one hoping for culinary trends.
'That's too salty!' someone may shout,
As the chef turns red and flails about.

Pasta twirls in a playful boil,
While sauces bubble in joyous toil.
We taco 'bout things too big to bite,
While desserts just want to take flight!

So let's flavor life with humor bright,
In every meal, find delight.
With laughter as the secret sauce,
Every dish wins, no matter the cost!

Flavors of the Forgotten

In the pantry, musty jars sit,
Lost flavors where memories split.
Forgotten spices, oh what a scene,
Pepper from times when kitchens were keen.

A dash of humor, a sprinkle of grit,
Mixing up meals, oh what a hit!
A pinch of this, a smidge of that,
Whisking up laughter, imagine that!

Eggs still in shades of years gone by,
Each one a story, oh me, oh my!
Pastas and sauces, a wild parade,
Feasting on quirks that time has made.

Digging for treasures, take out that spoon,
A buffet of giggles under the moon.
Let's taste our roots, with a side of fun,
Here's a dish made for everyone!

A Taste of Ancestry

Grandma's recipes, a marathon race,
Sticky fingers, flour on your face.
Cooking with love, and a pinch of sass,
A recipe book, that's sure to amass.

Measurements vague, just "a handful" here,
Laughter erupts, as we sneak in the beer.
A dash of this, a squirt of that,
Chasing our roots like a hungry rat.

Old family tales spice up the stew,
Ghosts in the kitchen might be cooking too!
Bubbling pots with secrets to share,
Creating a feast fit for a bear.

So grab your forks, and don't delay,
Ancestral flavors, come out to play!
Making a mess is half of the fun,
Together we snack till the morning sun!

Culinary Chronicles

Open the fridge, what will we see?
Leftovers dancing, begging for glee.
Last night's pizza, its glory is bright,
  It tells a tale of our midnight bite.

Silly soufflés and cakes falling flat,
Pasta disasters that looked like a cat.
Gourmet adventures, oh where do we start?
  Not every great chef has the perfect heart!

Sauces explode like silly confetti,
Chopping and dicing, the gang's all ready!
Flip that pancake, if it lands on the floor,
We'll scoop it up fast, and always want more.

So raise your spatulas, toast with your cups,
  Here's to the kitchen and all its hiccups!
Let's write our history in flour and spice,
  With laughter and fun, isn't that nice?

Harmony in Grains

In the world of grains, a tale unfolds,
Each one with secrets, waiting to be told.
Rice has a rhythm, and barley's got flair,
Let's dance with quinoa, if you dare!

Wheat loaves rising like bubbly balloons,
Flour cascades like enchanted dunes.
Mixing our whispers in a doughy embrace,
The symphony plays as we set the pace.

Oats serenade while millet takes flight,
Grains in a party, a marvelous sight.
Popping and crunching, so much delight,
They all come together, in a feast of sheer might.

So gather your grains, let's make it a blast,
In the harmony of meals, friendships are cast.
A sprinkle of laughter, a bite of cheer,
In the world of grains, our hearts feel near!

Tang of the Terra

In a world where spices clash,
Tomatoes dance, and peppers dash.
Garlic sneezes, onions cry,
While carrots giggle as they fly.

Cumin makes a funny face,
As ginger joins the lively race.
Together they form quite the team,
Cooking up a savory dream.

Parsley jumps, all fresh and bright,
A sprinkle here, a pinch of light.
From garden beds, they all unite,
Creating meals with pure delight.

So let's embrace this veggie crew,
In every color, every hue.
With laughter in each little bite,
A feast that feels just right tonight.

Taste of Tradition

A grandma's pot begins to bubble,
In the kitchen, there's no trouble.
With recipes passed down like gold,
Her secret chats with pots unfold.

Mmm, the scent of bread so warm,
It brings the family, safe from harm.
Each bite a hug, a cheerful grin,
A plate that whispers, "Come on in!"

Cousins joke as pasta twirls,
With olive oil and garlic swirls.
Stories simmer, laughter flows,
With every sprinkle, love still grows.

So grab your fork, don't be shy,
Let's share a meal and all comply.
In every dish, tradition thrives,
A taste of past where joy derives.

Unity in Diversity

Vegetables of every kind,
In one big pot, they're intertwined.
Peas and corn, they hold hands tight,
A rainbow stew, what a sight!

In this bowl, we laugh and cheer,
A sprinkle of joy, a dash of cheer.
From broccoli trees to carrot stars,
Mixing flavors from near and far.

Together they sing a silly song,
Potatoes and beans, they all belong.
With every bite, results are clear,
Diversity brings laughter here!

So scoop it up with a happy grin,
Let flavors mingle, let joy begin.
In every spoonful, tales unfold,
Cooking stories never grow old.

Harvesting Humanity

In fields so wide, we gather in,
Hands in dirt, a playful spin.
Veggies yelling, "Pick me, please!"
In a dance among the breeze.

Pumpkins chuckle, potatoes roll,
As cabbage twirls, now that's the goal!
Tomatoes winking bright and red,
A playful harvest, 'til we're fed.

From dawn till dusk, we sing and jest,
In laughter's warmth, we feel so blessed.
Each crop a joke, each leaf a grin,
Harvesting humanity, let's dive in!

So lift your fork, let laughter start,
In every meal, we share a part.
Together we munch, together we thrive,
Eating joy, we feel alive!

Fertile Blessings

In fields where carrots play hide and seek,
A potato dreams of being unique.
Squash rolls by, all plump and round,
While beets blush deeply, no chill to be found.

The corn whispers jokes to the breeze,
As peas giggle softly, feeling at ease.
Radishes turn redder with each silly pun,
While pumpkins bask, saying, "Aren't we the fun?"

Textures of Humanity

We're all just a mix of flavors and bites,
From spicy to sweet, with all of our fights.
A dash of humor in every cross word,
Crafting our lives with laughter absurd.

Some folks are smooth, while others are rough,
Like bread with its crust, we're all a bit tough.
But sprinkle some joy, and watch friendships thrive,
In this great potluck, where all are alive.

Wisdom in the Crust

Old bread once said, "I've seen it all,
From seeds to loaves, I've had quite the ball!
I've crumbled, I've toasted, and toasted again,
Life's just a slice; share it with friends!"

With cookies that crumble and tales that unfold,
Muffins sing tunes of adventures bold.
For every hard crust holds stories in light,
It's the flaky moments that make life just right.

Crystals of Existence

In a world where folks sparkle, a shimmer of fun,
Like sugar and salt when they join for a run.
Some days are diamonds, bright, and so clear,
Others are rough, but we cherish them dear.

Life's a mix of flavors, sweet and bizarre,
Sometimes we're rock candy, sometimes a tart star.
But look at us shine, through laughter and tears,
We're all just a recipe brewed through the years!

Grounded in Legacy

In dusty towns where laughter sings,
The grandmas tell of salty things.
They sprinkle tales, grain by grain,
Of recipes that drive us insane.

With shakers full of joy and glee,
They toss their spice like it's a spree.
A pinch of strange, a dash of bold,
Their kitchen magic never gets old.

From pancake flops to spaghetti slides,
They serve their love with giggling sides.
A table set with tales so grand,
Salt of wisdom in every hand.

We laugh and crunch on flavor's quest,
Each dish a quirky, tasty jest.
In every bite, a story's spun,
Our legacy, oh what fun we've done!

The Mineral Heart

Deep in the ground, where critters flee,
A mineral heart beats wild and free.
It giggles up from caves below,
Whispering secrets that make us glow.

With crystals bright and rocks that dance,
It crafts a rhythm, given the chance.
'Don't take life too serious!' it cries,
As diamonds wink from the earth's sly eyes.

Gravel roads where mischief thrives,
Underfoot, where silliness jives.
Smiling stones with a trickster's art,
Remind us all to play, not part.

So next you step on what feels plain,
Remember the laughter deep in the grain.
For even rocks have tales to tell,
In Earth's warm hug, we find our spell!

Essence Beneath Our Feet

With each step taken on this ground,
A tickle of humor can be found.
For underneath, where soil meets our shoes,
Silly sprites dance, bursting the blues.

The worms are busy, doing their jig,
While roots shake it, getting big.
'Don't step so hard!' they seem to squeal,
As dirt erupts like a fresh meal.

The ants conspire with winks and grins,
Digging tunnels like tiny wins.
Nature's jesters, playing for fun,
In every clod, the laughter is spun.

So dance a jig and stomp your feet,
Beneath our lives, the earth has beat.
A comedy show, right under our toes,
Where humor in nature endlessly grows!

Crystals of Resilience

In the rockiest places, they bloom and grow,
Crystals flashing, putting on a show.
Each facet tells a tale of cheer,
Of making it big from dust and fear.

Weathered and worn, they stand so tall,
'Hey, look at us! We won't fall!'
They twinkle bright in the night's embrace,
With every stumble, they find their place.

From grit to glamour, what a ride,
In the jewel of life, with joy as our guide.
A chuckle or two, as we shine through strife,
Even rock solid can have a funny life!

So raise your glass to the bold and clear,
The laughter and spark within us near.
Let's be like crystals, with hearts so bright,
Finding humor in all, our precious light!

Fundamental Seasoning

When life gets bland, just add some flair,
A pinch of laughter, lighten the air.
Forget about spice that's hoity-toity,
Simple salt makes everything quite hasty.

In the kitchen, see the chef go wild,
With clumps and grins, he's truly a child.
Dancing with jars, the spice flies high,
A sprinkle of joy makes the taste buds sigh.

Mix together flavors, don't shy away,
From sweet to sour, in a bold ballet.
Friends gather 'round with forks held tight,
Forking up laughs, it's a glorious sight.

So next time it's bland, and you're feeling low,
Remember the magic in the grains that glow.
Take a chance, spread cheer with each shake,
For life's just a dish, a giggle to bake.

A Palette of Grit

Life's a canvas, and we're the taste,
Gritty moments, never go to waste.
With laughter in brushstrokes, we paint the day,
A zing of zest in a playful way.

Sassy and salty, we flip the script,
From bland to bonkers, let humor be whipped.
A dash of nonsense, it adds to the fun,
With a mouthful of giggles, we're winning the run.

We gather like spices, from near and far,
Made stronger together, like a bizarre bazaar.
Stir in some mischief, a joyful blend,
In the art of laughter, we'll never end.

So bring on the grit, and let's taste the zest,
With friends by our side, we're truly the best.
Every palette we share, a savory treat,
In a world full of spice, we can't be beat.

The Flavor of Kinship

In the pot of life, we're all the spice,
Pairing our quirks like beans and rice.
Brothers and sisters, united we stand,
Seasoning moments, hand in hand.

A sprinkle of stories, shared and loud,
Gathered together, a merry crowd.
Tickle your taste buds, it's time to unwind,
With flavors of laughter, joy intertwined.

Stirring the brew, we find our groove,
Mixing our tales in a rhythmic move.
Friends orbit round like vegetables bright,
Creating connections, in sunshine and night.

So raise a toast with your favorite brew,
To kinship that sparkles with every chew.
For in this flavor, we find our mirth,
A banquet of love, the joy of our hearth.

Delicate Crystals of Courage

Tiny granules, each whisper of bold,
Sparkling like treasures, a story unfolds.
With every pinch that graces the dish,
Courage is seasoned, granting our wish.

Tiny crystals, so potent, so fine,
Bringing a giggle with every design.
We sprinkle on bravery with laughter's spark,
Creating a symphony, brightening the dark.

Gathered together, we dance and we sway,
With humor our compass, we'll light up the gray.
Just a dash of daring is all that we need,
To craft a new vision, plant a brave seed.

So crack open laughter, let courage take flight,
Seasoned with joy, we'll conquer the night.
In delicate crystals, our spirits will shine,
For courage and humor are wonderfully entwined.

From Soil to Spirit

In fields of clods and jests, we toil,
With laughter sprouting from the soil.
We dance with worms and chuckle bright,
As carrots play hide and seek with light.

The cows wear shades, the pigs all sing,
A bubbling brook, a jolly fling.
With every turn of hoe and spade,
We dig for jokes that won't soon fade.

When harvest comes, we throw a feast,
In laughter's grip, we find our beast.
The corn it pops, in buttery cheer,
With ears that listen, grin from ear to ear.

So here's to soil, with all its mirth,
A spirit high, we bless the earth.
With humor's grit, we'll plant our schemes,
And rise anew in fluffy dreams.

Crust of Experience

A loaf of life, we knead and roll,
With every slice, we find our soul.
The crust is tough, but oh, it's grand,
With crumbs of laughter close at hand.

The yeast of joy begins to rise,
Baking tales beneath the skies.
A sprinkle here, a pinch of wit,
In every bite, the world we slit.

The butter spreads, the jam does dance,
On toast of dreams, we take our chance.
With each new spread, a story swells,
In cozy kitchens, laughter tells.

So raise a slice to seasoned years,
With crusty laughs and joyful cheers.
For every crumb holds tales to share,
In love and loaf, we find our dare.

Whispers of the Land

The breeze it tickles through the trees,
With secrets murmured, sweet as peas.
A dancing leaf, a chuckling brook,
Nature's humor in every nook.

The daisies gossip, the potatoes grin,
While squirrels plot their next great win.
Each blade of grass spins tales of old,
With giggles wrapped in shades of gold.

The sun winks down, the clouds all tease,
A playful game among the leaves.
With every gust, a snicker finds,
In nature's charm, the heart unwinds.

So listen close and take a cue,
From whispers soft that bring us new.
In every rustle, laughter grows,
In nature's jest, our joy bestows.

Layers of Memory

In jars of time, we pickle dreams,
With laughter bubbling at the seams.
Each layer thick, with stories bright,
We feast on flavors, day and night.

The onions weep, the garlic smiles,
As memories linger through the miles.
A dash of spice, a sprinkle of glee,
Finds joy in the mundane, you see.

We bottle up the laughs we've shared,
With every taste, our hearts are bared.
From salsa thick to soup divine,
Each bite a moment, laughter's wine.

So toast the layers, rich and bold,
In every jar, a memory told.
With every nibble, time unwinds,
In flavors deep, our joy one finds.

Flavors of the Land

A sprinkle of garlic, a dash of thyme,
Makes even the bland feel like a rhyme.
On this plate, we dance and twirl,
Laughter spices up every swirl.

Basil on pizza, a hug from the sauce,
Every bite makes us feel like a boss.
Spuds in the oven, all golden and crisp,
Who needs a diet when you've got this lisp?

Essential Harvest

Plucked from the earth, our veggies cheer,
Radishes jive, while carrots just sneer.
Eggplants gossip, so juicy and bold,
Telling the tales of their ripening gold.

Tomatoes burst in a fit of delight,
Ketchup dreams take off in flight.
Garlic and onions, a duo so grand,
Making us weep, but we still eat planned!

Seasons of Seasoning

Winter brings spices, a cozy delight,
Cinnamon dances with nutmeg all night.
Spring's fresh herbs twirl in the sun,
A pesto party has just begun!

Summer's a fiesta, with heat in the air,
Chilies and limes, we spice up with flair.
Fall brings the pumpkins, so ranging and round,
Harvest that humor, it's a joyous sound!

Savoring the Soil

From dirt to plate, a wild journey starts,
Each veggie's story tugs at our hearts.
We giggle and munch, as flavors collide,
In this riot of taste, we take a ride.

The earth's little treasures, how quirky they are,
Zucchini's a noodle; did you go too far?
With jest in each bite, we relish our fate,
A banquet of giggles, we celebrate!

Weaving Earth and Soul

In fields where laughter grows tall,
We dance with joy, we stumble and fall.
We sprinkle humor like seeds in the air,
Mixing our sorrows with comic flair.

Oh, the dirt has a charm that's hard to beat,
With worms doing jiggles in summer's heat.
Each pebble a punchline, each root a joke,
Nature's own circus—oh, what a poke!

As we dig our toes in the soft earthy muck,
Our hearts are as full as an old pickup truck.
We gather around, sharing tales and grins,
Like carrots in hats—oh, let the fun begin!

In this playful patchwork, we find our way,
With laughter our shovel, we dig every day.
Planting our dreams in the tilled, warm ground,
In the comedy garden, true joys abound!

Tasteful Threads

In every bite of pie, there's a story to tell,
Like grandma's old recipes kissed by a spell.
We sprinkle some giggles, a dash of delight,
Turning bland meals into festive delight!

With spices that tickle and herbs that cheer,
We feast on the humor that brings us near.
Life's tablecloth wrinkled, but so full of cheer,
Each course served with laughter, oh what a year!

A pinch of mischief, a spoonful of cheer,
Our table's a stage—come join, never fear!
With forks made of fun and plates stacked with jest,
Each moment a bite that's the very best!

So gather your friends, let's toast with a grin,
To flavors of laughter, where joy does begin.
In the kitchen of life, we bake up our fate,
With heartfelt connections, it's never too late!

Underlying Richness

Under the surface, the quirks come alive,
Like potatoes in boots, we dance and we jive.
Roots wrapped in laughter, we dig deep and smile,
Finding joy in the quirks, it's truly our style.

The Earth's got a rhythm, a beat we can feel,
With goofy old gophers who try to conceal.
They dig out the punchlines, we laugh from the dirt,
In the garden of life, humor grows where we flirt.

Every grain holds a giggle, each stone has a jest,
Our harvest of laughs is the truest, the best.
With shovels of humor and rakes made of mirth,
We'll dig up the treasures awaiting our birth.

So join in the frolic, let earthworms unite,
In the soil of our hearts, everything feels right.
For what's underneath isn't just mud and clay,
It's a tapestry woven with laughter each day!

Craving Connection

In a world full of flavors, we search for a taste,
A sprinkle of friendship, not one bit of waste.
We dine on nostalgia, with each hearty laugh,
Sharing bits of our stories, a culinary path.

As flavors combine in the pot of our dreams,
We're making a stew, or so it seems.
With each shared moment, we mix up our fates,
A recipe brewing—oh, can't you relate?

So pass me a tater, I'll share you a grin,
In this grand kitchen, let the fun begin!
From snacks to our chats, let's savor the blend,
For bonds are the spices, they never will end.

Let's feast on connection, raise glasses so high,
To flavors of laughter that never run dry.
With hearty good humor, our table's complete,
In this banquet of life, we've all got a seat!

Bound by Flavor

In a land where pickles dance,
And spices giggle with a glance,
The pepper sneezes, oh what a sight,
As salt shimmies, ready for a fight.

Garlic whispers tales so bold,
While onions cry, or so I'm told,
The cumin chuckles, adding glee,
In this odd kitchen jamboree.

Thyme is laughing, what a tease!
Oregano joins with zest and ease,
Together they frolic, a flavorful team,
Creating dishes that make you dream.

So next time you sauté or bake,
Remember to dance before you take,
For in every bite, a story waits,
A sprinkle of joy upon your plates.

Epochs of Earth

Long ago, in a garden bright,
Potatoes plotted under moonlight,
Carrots grinned and made a pact,
To rule the plates in a veggie act.

Tomatoes taught them how to red,
While lettuce rolled its eyes and said,
"Oh, here we go, the show begins,
As chefs tune in for all our sins!"

Cabbage tells jokes in leafy tones,
While broccoli flexes, showing its bones,
The squash, a comedian in its own right,
Cracks up the mushrooms, what a delight!

In nature's cabaret, they sing and play,
Defying the norm in a veggie ballet,
So chop with a laugh, and sauté with flair,
This garden of joy is beyond compare!

Aromatic Echoes

Whiffs of garlic tickle my nose,
As basil hums in leafy prose,
Peppercorns giggle on the rack,
Spilling secrets of the flavor pack.

An onion chops, shedding tears of joy,
They all agree that spice is no ploy,
"Let's turn up the heat!" the ginger cries,
As nutmeg nods with twinkling eyes.

Chili flames with fiery jokes,
While bay leaves sway like dancing folks,
In every pot a party brews,
With laughter bubbling in a fragrant muse.

So bring out your pans and cutlery, too,
The banquet awaits, come join the crew,
For in every meal, a chuckle awaits,
A feast of aromas that celebrates!

Flora's Fingerprint

In a garden where herbs wear crowns,
Thyme throws confetti; sage never frowns,
Rosemary struts in a flowery dress,
While mint pulls pranks with a leafy finesse.

Dandelions shout, "We're not weeds!"
With every bloom, they plant their seeds,
Chives roll their eyes, while herbs unite,
Creating a party that feels just right.

Cilantro's fresh; it brings the groove,
As parsley cousins do the moonwalk move,
Their laughter rings through the sunlit air,
Flora's fingerprint, a whimsical flair.

So plant some humor in your garden plot,
Let nature's antics be your cooking pot,
For in every leaf, a chuckle resides,
A dash of fun where flavor abides.

Grains of Wisdom

A sprinkle here and a dash there,
Shakers giggle, they spread in the air.
Life tastes better, oh what a treat,
But watch out, don't slip on your feet!

In the kitchen, we gather 'round,
With stories and laughter, joy is found.
Sprinkling wisdom over our bread,
Don't ask for too much, or you'll end up dead!

From chefs to kids, we all agree,
A grain of salt makes a life so free.
Remember the times it slips from hands,
Creating giggles and culinary bands!

So let's toast with our glasses raised high,
To grains of wisdom that never run dry.
A dash of laughter, a pinch of zest,
In the world of bland, we'll always be blessed!

Essence of Dust

In corners where shadows love to dance,
Lies the essence of a speck of chance.
Dust bunnies giggle, they're secretly proud,
Whispering tales, quite loud and avowed.

Each film we swipe gives a glimpse of fun,
A staining joke under the morning sun.
A sneeze escapes, and the laughter erupts,
Though we all know that the cleaning's corrupt.

From floors to shelves, it adds to the charm,
A sprinkle of chaos that brings no alarm.
It's part of our lives, this powdery bliss,
In every small speck, there's a moment not missed!

With each little swirl, we'll dance in delight,
The essence of dust makes our day bright.
So here's to the particles, funny and light,
In a world that's spotless, we wouldn't take flight!

Flavors of the Ground

A kick from the earth, oh, what a thrill!
With a crunch and a munch, let's feast 'til we spill.
Potatoes and carrots, all mixed with glee,
Flavors of the ground, as fun as can be!

With veggies that giggle and grains full of cheer,
We cook them together, the laughter draws near.
Mashing and dicing, it's all quite a show,
Who knew humus could bring such a glow?

From dirt to our plates, it's a daring ride,
With flavors so funky, we eat with pride.
Salads that dance, and sauces that sing,
In the garden of laughter, we find everything!

So when you think food, consider the earth,
Each bite brings joy, a blossoming birth.
With a pinch of fun and a dash of delight,
Let's savor the flavors, oh what a sight!

Saline Echoes

With a sprinkle of joy, we gather our crew,
For echoes of laughter in waves of blue.
Shaking our shakers, we douse the dish,
Who knew a simple salt could grant every wish?

In kitchens where moments become little songs,
We add just a pinch, righting all the wrongs.
Echoes of seasoning, a flavor parade,
In the Kingdom of Snacks, it's the salt that we grade!

Hear conversations, seasoned with cheer,
From fish to popcorn, it's music we hear.
In laughter and joy, we sprinkle and share,
With every bite taken, it's love in the air!

So let the echoes of flavor resound,
With salty surprises, let laughter abound.
In every good meal, let's cherish and toast,
To the simple joys, of which we can boast!

Terra's Diamond

In the garden, worms do dance,
Composting nonsense, give it a chance.
Radishes wiggle, peas play peek,
Claiming the sun, a humorous streak.

Beets in their coats, all dressed to impress,
They hold a party, but who would guess?
Carrots are rappers, they drop it like it's hot,
And turnips just giggle, I kid you not!

The daisies all gossip, the dandelions tease,
While broccoli's busy with its greens to please.
Fungi are prancing, spreading the cheer,
Nature's own circus, let's grab a beer!

So cherish this soil, with laughter it thrives,
A comedy show where every plant strives.
In nature's own humor, life finds its cheer,
A playful reminder, let's all volunteer!

Gastronomic Footprints

Garlic and onions, they strut down the lane,
Hiring tomatoes to join in their reign.
With peppers all salsa, they move to the beat,
Creating a banquet that's hard to defeat.

Cabbage rolls in, with a swagger so bold,
While mushrooms do flips, their stories unfold.
Zucchini plays tag, running wild and free,
A food truck parade, come taste the glee!

This veggie brigade brings laughter and zest,
Every bite's a giggle, a culinary fest.
Eggplants wear capes, peas sing out loud,
In this funny feast, you'll be quite proud!

So grab a fork, let the humor overflow,
Savor the laughter that food can bestow.
With flavors that tickle and textures that tease,
A kitchen adventure, that's sure to please!

Underfoot Treasures

Down in the dirt, what do we find?
A giggling potato, oh what a kind!
It wiggles and jigs, in the soil so deep,
Dreams of being mashed, but first, take a peek!

Radish reports of wormy debates,
They wriggle and squabble, and chatter their fates.
A carrot with style, in a jaunty green hat,
Says, 'Join my parade, oh how cool is that!'

Underneath all, there's a comedy scene,
With beet actors strutting, they set the routine.
A treasure of laughter lies low to the ground,
In the clumps of the earth, pure joy can be found!

So dig up those giggles and share them around,
In each quirky root, there's laughter profound.
Celebrate life in its earthy display,
With humor embedded beneath every layer!

Echoes of Fertility

The seedlings shout, 'We're here for a show!'
With nutty ambitions they're ready to grow.
Chickpeas crack jokes, while lentils just beam,
Together they laugh, like a wild, funny dream.

In the breeze, they sway, choreographing their fate,
As cucumbers gossip, saying, 'Aren't we great?'
While sunflowers pose, striking a pose,
Giving high-fives to the squash on their toes!

The heart of the earth knows how to provide,
With sprouts of amusement, let laughter collide.
A festival blooms, with nature in tow,
In the echoes of life, it's a humorous show!

So let's cheer for the groove, take a moment to play,
With giggling gardens that brighten the day.
In fields of fertility, where joy never ends,
We dance with the earth and call it good friends!

Culinary Roots

In the garden, weeds take flight,
While carrots dream of chasing light.
A radish wears a fancy suit,
While potatoes play the hide-and-scoot.

Garlic bulbs, with breath so bold,
Claiming tales of flavor untold.
Onions cry, but don't you fret,
They're not the worst to make a bet.

Tomatoes blush with summer's kiss,
In recipes that can't be missed.
Meanwhile, lettuce tends to pout,
When dressed too soon, it voices doubt.

But in this patch, our laughter grows,
With veggies dancing, strike a pose.
So slice and dice, let flavors sing,
In culinary roots, we'll find our zing.

Tides of Flavor

Waves of broth are rolling in,
A fishy tale begins to swim.
Seaweed giggles, tosses curls,
While shrimp compete for best of pearls.

Garlic butter breaks the scene,
Mussels party, oh so keen!
Crab legs wave, they're feeling fine,
While clams just sip on brine and wine.

The beach brings sand, the grill brings cheer,
Charred remains from last week's beer.
A seagull swoops for fries with a grunt,
As we all savor every front.

So raise a glass, to seas and feasts,
With tides of flavor, laughter beasts.
We'll feast and dance till the sun's delight,
In kitchens bright, our spirits light.

Aromas of the Soil

In dirt we trust, where flavors sprout,
With herbs that whisper, and greens that shout.
Parsley prances, basil bows,
While thyme and sage share cooking vows.

Tomato plants throw shade and laughs,
As radishes tell their funny drafts.
Carrots giggle underground,
While beets just blush without a sound.

A spud named Chuck claims he's a star,
Growing tales of journeys far.
"Chips and fries are just the start,
But mashed, I'll break your cooking heart!"

So let the garden sing its tune,
With aromas rising, mornings' boon.
In nature's soil, the laughter brews,
Flavor's roots have plenty to choose!

Subtle Savors

Subtle hints in each bite await,
Like a secret dance on a dinner plate.
A sprinkle here, a dash of sass,
Cooking up jokes that make us laugh!

Peppers poke with spicy glee,
While mustard's up for a friendly spree.
Vinegar swoops in, a cheeky grin,
Creating chaos in the din.

Herbs like rebels, fresh and bold,
Whisper stories of flavors old.
Chili flakes join in the fray,
Bringing heat to spice the play.

So gather 'round, taste buds cheer,
With subtle savors drawing near!
In laughter's feast, we find our groove,
It's food and fun that makes us move.

Earthbound Treasure

In the dirt, we dig and sweep,
Finding gems where critters creep.
Beneath our feet, a world's delight,
Silly treasures, hidden from sight.

A potato, proud, wears a crown,
While a carrot's the joker in town.
Turnips telling jokes, oh what fun,
In this patch, we've all just won!

Frogs in hats and worms that dance,
Each oddball creature gets a chance.
Laughter spills from every hole,
In this earthy, quirky role.

So if you walk and see a mound,
Just dig a bit, joy will abound.
For every root, a smile hides,
In the soil where laughter abides.

Unseen Flavors of Life

Life's spices are tossed with flair,
Invisible flavors fill the air.
Garlic's giggle, onion's tease,
Every bite, a tasty sneeze!

Best friends in the pot, a curry song,
Each ingredient where they belong.
A dash of this and a sprinkle of that,
Cooking up joy, it's where it's at!

Peppers dance to a sizzling beat,
While beans mingle, oh so sweet.
Earth's pantry packed with clever glee,
Who knew radishes could be so free?

Taste buds tickle, laughter flows,
As avocados strike funny poses.
With each bite, a chuckle awakens,
Delicious life, where joy's not mistaken!

Essence of Existence

In a world that loves to play,
Life's essence giggles in a way.
From silly ants to the bees' tease,
Nature's comedy, brought to its knees.

Dancing leaves in a sprinkler's mist,
Even the grass can't resist!
Sunflowers strut in the golden light,
While squirrels have tea, oh what a sight!

Clouds lumber by, making a scene,
Like fluffy pillows, proud and mean.
"Catch us if you can!" they jest,
In the sky, they humorously rest.

Every raindrop, a giggle's cheer,
The essence of life, oh so dear!
For in each moment, laughter's the key,
To the joy of being wild and free.

Savory Footprints

Paw prints, hoof prints, all around,
A savory trail where fun is found.
Each little mark tells a tale,
Of mischief made on the grassy trail.

A cat's pirouette, the dog's big leap,
Footprints in the mud, oh so deep.
Chasing the wind, they leave behind,
Giggles that linger, joy intertwined.

Little critters with big shoes to fill,
Making footprints that give us a thrill.
In the kitchen of life, they feast and play,
Cooking up fun in their own clever way.

So watch the path where the laughter leads,
With every step, a new joy feeds.
Savory stories in every stride,
As the world walks on, united with pride.

www.ingramcontent.com/pod-product-compliance
Lightning Source LLC
Chambersburg PA
CBHW072215070526
44585CB00015B/1344